You Shall Not Have Strange Gods Before Me

Reflections on the Commandments

Joseph Anfossi and John Villata

Pauline
ST. PAUL BOOKS & MEDIA

Nihil Obstat:
Very Rev. Timothy J. Shea, VF

Imprimatur:
✠Bernard Cardinal Law

January 5, 1995

Photo credits: FSP 14; Kevin Galvin 30; Vincent Mancusi 35; Visual Horizons 38; St. Paul International 43

Design by Mary Joseph Peterson, FSP

ISBN: 0-8198-8801-X

Original title: *Non avrai altro dio di fronte a me*

Original series title: *Note sulle "dieci parole"*

Translated from the Italian by Mary James Berger, FSP

Printed and published in the U.S.A. by Pauline Books & Media, 50 St. Paul's Avenue, Boston, MA 02130.

Pauline Books & Media is the publishing house of the Daughters of St. Paul, an international congregation of women religious serving the Church with the communications media.

1 2 3 4 5 99 98 97 96 95

CONTENTS

INTRODUCTION

This contemporary European Christmas story is a good lead-in to the theme of this booklet.

The ancient Gothic cathedral is gloomy...with such a web of chapels and sacristies that, after centuries of neglect, some haven't yet been explored. What will the lean archbishop do on Christmas night—people asked—all alone, while the city is celebrating? How will he be able to overcome melancholy? Everyone has some consolation: the baby has a train and a Pinocchio, his sister has a doll, the mother has her children around her, the sick person has new hope, the old bachelor has a leisure companion, the prisoner has the voice of the person in the next cell. What will the archbishop do? The zealous Fr. Valentine, secretary to His Excellency, smiled when he heard the people talking like that. The archbishop has God on Christmas night. Kneeling all alone in the cold, deserted cathedral, at first sight he might make you feel sorry for him, but instead, if you only knew! He's not alone, he's not even cold, and he doesn't feel abandoned. On Christmas night God fills the temple for the archbishop; the aisles literally overflow with his presence, so much so that the doors don't want to remain closed. And, though there are no heaters, it's so warm that the old white snakes awaken in the tombs of the abbots and ascend through the air vents from the cellar, to gently stick their heads out the balustrades of the confessionals.

That's what the cathedral was like that evening: filled with God. And even though he knew it wasn't his duty, Fr. Valentine was only too willing to arrange the bishop's kneeler. Never mind Christmas trees, turkeys and gushing wine! This was a Christmas night. While lost in these thoughts, he heard someone knocking at a door. "Who's knocking at the door of the cathedral on Christmas night?" Fr. Valentine asked himself. "Haven't they prayed enough?

What madness has come over them?" While he was saying this, he went to open the door, and with a rush of wind a poor man clothed in rags came in.

"How much presence of God there is here!" the poor man exclaimed smiling, looking around. "How beautiful! You can feel it even outside. Monsignor, couldn't you let me have a little? After all, it's Christmas night."

"It belongs to His Excellency the archbishop," the priest answered. "He'll be here in a couple of hours. His Excellency already leads the life of a saint; I'd never expect him to renounce God too! And then, I've never been a monsignor."

"Not even a little bit, Reverend Father? There's so much! His Excellency would not even notice!"

"I said no.... You can leave.... The cathedral is closed to the public." And he sent the poor man away with ten dollars.

But at the same moment the man left the church, God disappeared. Dismayed, Fr. Valentine looked around, examining the dark vaults. God wasn't even up there. The spectacular array of columns, statues, altars, candelabra and drapery, usually so mysterious and powerful, had suddenly become sinister and inhospitable. And in a few hours the archbishop would be coming.

Flustered and upset, Fr. Valentine opened one of the outside doors and looked out onto the square. Nothing. Even outside, although it was Christmas, there was no sign of God. Echoes of laughter, breaking glasses, music and even blasphemies came from the thousand lighted windows. No bells, no hymns.

Fr. Valentine went out into the night. He walked through the profane streets, amidst the din of wild feasting. However, he knew the right address. When he entered the house, the family members were seating themselves at table. They were all looking kindly at one another, and around them there was a bit of the presence of God.

"Merry Christmas, Father," said the head of the house. "Will you join us?"

"I'm in a hurry, my friends," he answered. "Through my carelessness, God has abandoned the cathedral, and soon His Excellency will be going there to pray. Can you give me yours? Indeed, you are company to one another, and you don't really need him."

"My dear Father Valentine," replied the father. "You are forgetting that today is Christmas. Should my children be without God on this day? I'm surprised at you, Fr. Valentine."

At the very moment the man was saying this, God rushed out of the room. The happy smiles disappeared and the roasted chicken felt like sand in their mouths.

Out he went again, into the night. Fr. Valentine walked and walked along the deserted streets until he saw God again. He had reached the gates of the city, and in front of him the wide countryside extended into the darkness, whitened somewhat by the snow. Over the fields and the rows of mulberry bushes, God was hovering, as if waiting. Fr. Valentine fell on his knees.

"What are you doing, Father?" a farmer asked. "Do you want to get sick in this cold weather?"

"Look there, my son. Don't you see?"

The farmer looked without surprise. "He's ours," he said. "Every Christmas he comes to bless our fields."

"Listen," said the priest, "couldn't you give me some? In the city we are without God. Even the churches are empty. Let me have a little so that our archbishop can at least have a decent Christmas."

"But don't even suggest it, my dear Father. Who knows what horrible sins you've committed in your city. It's your fault. Take care of yourselves."

"Certainly, we've sinned. And who doesn't? But you can save many souls, my son, if you only say yes."

"I have enough worry saving mine!" the farmer retorted. At the moment he said that, God left his fields and disappeared into the darkness.

The priest went on and on, looking. God seemed to make himself more and more scarce, and those who possessed something of God didn't want to give it up (but at the very moment they answered no, God disappeared, withdrawing into the distance).

Finally Fr. Valentine reached the borders of a very vast moorland. In the background, on the horizon, God shone sweetly like a cloud. The priest fell on his knees in the snow. "Wait for me, Lord!" he begged. "It's my fault the archbishop is alone, and tonight is Christmas!"

He had frozen feet, he walked in the fog, he was up to his knees in snow, every so often he would stumble and fall. How long could he go on?

Then he heard a distant, impassioned choir, the voices of angels; a ray of light filtered through the fog. He opened a small wooden door: it was a huge church, and in the middle of it, surrounded by lights, a priest was praying. And the church was filled with paradise.

"Brother," cried Fr. Valentine, at the end of his strength, bristling with icicles, "have pity on me. Through my fault, the archbishop is alone and needs God. Give me some, I beg you."

Slowly the priest who was praying turned toward him. And Fr. Valentine, recognizing him, became even more pale—if that were possible.

"Merry Christmas to you, Fr. Valentine," exclaimed the archbishop, coming to meet him, surrounded by God. "My dear young man, where did you go? May I know what you went to look for on a night like this?"[1]

This thought-provoking contemporary tale brings us into our topic: a stimulating exploration of the mystery of the "God of Abraham, of Isaac and of Jacob," and of his claim to be the only God, as the first commandment says (Ex 20:2-3).

Overview

You Shall Not Have Strange Gods Before Me

What idols prevent today's people from penetrating the mystery of the God who cannot be made someone's "possession"?

The first two sections of this booklet are dedicated to the problem:

God cannot bear rivals

We each think of God in our own way.

The relevance of the topic leads to a number of well-articulated viewpoints. These are intended to help the reader mature a personal faith that can overcome the temptation to "possess" God and thus give in to idolatry.

Finally, there is the story of Edith Stein, a Hebrew woman who became an atheist during her earlier years of study but was always open to the search for truth. While developing her intellectual life, she let herself be penetrated by the mystery of the God of Jesus Christ.

TOPICS

The God Who Created You Is a Jealous God

The Lord says: "I am a jealous God."
Should this surprise us?
Should he have said: "I am an indifferent God"?
Like all persons in love, God cannot bear rivals;
he gives great importance to our fidelity,
which we should continually ask for in prayer
and which we receive in adoration.
In prayer, the Christian bases his or her whole life on God;
in adoration, unifies the heart;
in silence communicates with the loved one;
in praise and jubilation, opens the heart wide.[2]

God Cannot Bear Rivals

The Bible narrates that the Israelites were tired of waiting for Moses. Forty days and forty nights had already passed since he had climbed Sinai, the mountain to which the Lord had called him to give him the "tables of stone, with the law and the commandment..." (Ex 24:12).

They turned to Aaron and said: "'Up, make us gods, who shall go before us; as for this Moses, the man who brought us up out of the land of Egypt, we do not know what has become of him.'

"And Aaron said to them, 'Take off the rings of gold which are in the ears of your wives, your sons, and your daughters, and bring them to me.' So all the people took off the rings of gold which were in their ears, and brought them to Aaron. And he received the gold at their hand, and fashioned it with a graving tool, and made a molten calf; and they said, 'These are your gods, O Israel, who brought you up out of the land of Egypt!' When Aaron saw this, he built an altar before it; and Aaron made proclamation and said, 'Tomorrow shall be a feast to the Lord.'" And so it was.

The "calf" was a young bull, a symbol in the ancient east of strength and fertility.

God informed Moses about what had happened and told him to go down in haste because the people he had led out of slavery to freedom "have corrupted themselves.... They have made for themselves a molten calf, and have worshiped it and sacrificed to it, and said, 'These are your gods, O Israel, who brought you up out of the land of Egypt!'"

Then, the Bible continues, the Lord—who was indignant and angry over this—added: "I have seen this people, and behold it is a stiff-necked people."

With difficulty Moses succeeded in calming God's wrath and went down the mountain. He walked toward the camp, carrying the "two tables of the testimony in his hands.... As soon as he came near the camp and saw the calf and the dancing, Moses' anger burned hot, and he threw the tables out of his hands and broke them at the foot of the mountain. And he took the calf that they had made, and burnt it with fire, and ground it to powder, and scattered it upon the water, and made the people of Israel drink it" (Ex 32:1-20).

Idolatry—a recurring temptation

Without doubt, one of the strongest temptations, if not *the* strongest, the people of the covenant had to struggle against was that of idolatry.

In a certain sense, "the Bible is the story of the people detaching itself from idols."[3]

Here are some examples of this:

Eve agrees with the serpent, who puts a "great idea" into her head: "You will not die. For God knows that when you eat of it your eyes will be opened, and you will be like God, knowing good and evil" (Gen 3:4).

The history of the Hebrew people begins with the Lord's proposal to Abraham, the man who would become the "father of all believers," who was called by God while he worshiped other gods (cf. Gen 12).

The prophets insistently admonish the people not to forget the event of the golden calf. Let's recall what Jeremiah wrote, when he said in God's name, "What wrong did your ancestors find in me that they went far from me, and went after worthlessness, and became worthless?" (2:5) And further on, God reproaches Israel with its ingratitude: "Yet I planted you a choice vine, wholly of pure seed. How then have you turned degenerate and become a wild vine?" (2:21)

In the New Testament, too, the temptation to turn to

idols rather than to the true God takes a heavy toll of victims.

Paul urges the citizens of Thessalonica to continue to walk on the way of the Lord, so that it might always be said that they "turned to God from idols, to serve a living and true God" (1 Thess 1:9). To the Corinthians he repeats: "Therefore, my beloved, shun the worship of idols.... I do not want you to be partners with demons. You cannot drink the cup of the Lord and the cup of demons [the pagan gods]. You cannot partake of the table of the Lord and the table of demons. Shall we provoke the Lord to jealousy? Are we stronger than he?" (1 Cor 10:14-22)

The history of the Church, in which the struggle between Jesus and the "world" continues, has been marked by the temptation to adore the image of the beast (cf. Rev 13:14; 16:2), to accept what has been placed in the temple—as the prophet Daniel records—"the desolating sacrilege" (Mt 24:15).

Against what God?

Idolatry, then, isn't an easy temptation to overcome, especially once and for all. It appears in different forms. No sooner does one cease to serve the Lord, then one becomes the slave of every sort of "master": money (Mt 6:24); wine (Titus 2:3); will to dominate others (Col 3:5; Eph 5:5); political power (Rev 13:8); pleasure, envy and hatred (Rom 6:19); the stomach (Phil 3:19); sin (Rom 6:6); and even observance of the law when one's heart is not in it (Gal 4:8ff).

Who is the God that we sin against by idolatry?

We will resume the discussion begun in the first booklet. It's necessary to know well the God whom we serve or leave.

The God of the Covenant—the One, the Holy

The image of God that the Old Testament offers us can be outlined in three characteristics that are tightly bound together.

The first: God is the living God, that is, the God of the promises, of the covenant, of the exodus. He is the father, the spouse. This is how Israel immediately perceived him. The active God, standing beside his people, asks his people to "remain his" and to give him unconditional assent.

The second: God is the only God, that is, the only God who saves us. All other gods are nothing, and he reduces to nothing those who prefer other gods to him.

The third characteristic justifies and completes the other two. If God is our Savior (he is the living God) and is the only one who can truly be God (God alone is God), it is because he is radically different from us. God is the Holy One; he is spirit; he is strength and power without limit. The human person, instead, is lack—that is, transient weakness, like the grass that withers or like the passing of a bird in flight.

Yet, though God is so totally other, he is not distant from us.

God—the Father of Jesus

The otherness of God has been truly given to humanity. It is not seen only to be hidden again. It is expressed in a concrete person: Jesus of Nazareth.

Jesus assumes the image of God proposed by the Old Testament; he confirms it completely, he frees it from the suffocating influence of the pharisaic spirit. He so enlarges this image that it becomes, while remaining the same, completely new and unedited.

For Jesus, God is the living One, the only God, the Holy One, but above all he is Father. However, Jesus does not

only state that God is Father but—and herein lies the "new and unedited" part—he reveals how far this fatherhood reaches.

God is not a hindrance, as some modern masters of doubt insinuate (cf. the Views sections). God is not distant from real life; he is not irrelevant; neither is he harmful, as some may seriously think.

He is instead the God who stands at our origin, who accompanies us during the span of our lives and welcomes us at the point of arrival as our true destination and fullness.

He entrusts the entire universe to us because he wants us to resemble him and be his sons and daughters.

We are "like God" when we do not passively enjoy the fruits of others' creativity but become active creators of our own destiny—when we assume our responsibilities without waiting for solutions to fall from heaven; and finally, when we follow the way of the cross. We cannot, in fact, enter into the fatherhood of God if we don't abandon our own ideologies and self-sufficiency.

The consequences

When renewing the covenant after the "episode" of the golden calf, the Lord repeats: "You shall worship no other god, for the Lord, whose name is Jealous, is a jealous God" (Ex 34:14).

So God and idols can't stay together.

"You shall not have other gods besides me," the Lord proclaimed on Sinai. The commandment asks people of every age to remain what they are, creatures made in the image of God who is Father, living as responsible sons and daughters, without overturning the order of creation.

Otherwise, instead of becoming freer and contributing to liberation, we become slaves of other masters; instead of contributing to joy and happiness, we are forced to make enormous sacrifices to maintain our own idols; and in the end, we derive nothing positive or truly useful for ourselves or for others.

Idols are not only unproductive but they create anxiety and the fear of losing the object of one's desire.

We Each Think of God in Our Own Way

History tells us that human beings have always had different names for God. In the West, where Christian language prevails, we use the word "God" and its equivalents, but every religion has its own term.

Is the diversity of terms only a linguistic problem, or does it raise again the old temptation to make a "golden calf," that is, a "god," with one's own hands?

On the way toward the mystery

"I remember what a missionary friend told me in northern Kenya," writes an author who has a profound knowledge of world religions. "After he had spent days digging in the desert in search of water, a wet layer of rock crunched under the pickax and water sprang out of the crevice. 'Stop,' yelled the man who was helping him, 'the first water is for "Waqua," the god who gives the rain.'

"I think of the elderly Hindu man, who took care of the garden at the Catholic seminary in Nagpur, in the heart of India. When the sun rose, he sat in the 'lotus position' to celebrate his daily sacrifice, offering a handful of rice and a small banana to the all-powerful Shiva, giver of life. I see the trestles of the fields of Bali covered with flower petals and fresh buds to keep the evil spirits away from the rice harvest. I find myself with the elderly African man who, before offering me milk on the threshold of his manyatta, pours some drops out onto the ground as a gift to his ancestors. I relive the scene of that Moslem man and woman in the vineyards of Urgup in Turkey.... They prostrated themselves on the ground in the ritual of the *raka'at,* to pray to the omnipotent and merciful Allah.

"I see once again the young Japanese mother who bowed deeply several times in front of the image of Kwannon. Then she gently bent the head of the child in her arm, in homage to the sacred image. I think of the crowds at Benares who immerse themselves in the sacred waters of the Ganges, and rub their eyes with it to obtain purification and light. I find myself with millions of pilgrims who have come from all over India. They camp in the valley where the Ganges meets the Yamuna, near Allahabad, to immerse themselves in the waters on the night of the feast of *Kumba mela*. They hope to obtain absolution of all their faults. I see the gathering of the Jews at the wailing wall in Jerusalem, praying, swaying so as to give God the homage of their whole body. I think of the crowds at all the Marian shrines throughout the world."[4]

Every city on earth has its religious buildings, every village has its church or mosque or pagoda or sacred ediface, a space to which the heart turns spontaneously; a sign of the existence of "something greater" which each person has deeply rooted in their heart, and which can't help but express itself, even though in a variety of forms.

The Second Vatican Council recognizes this "constant something that cannot be done away with" in the "unsolved riddles of the human condition, which today, even as in former times, deeply stir the hearts of men: What is man? What is the meaning, the aim of our life? What is moral good, what is sin? Where does suffering come from and what purpose does it serve? Which is the road to true happiness? What are death, judgment, and retribution after death? What, finally, is that ultimate inexpressible mystery which encompasses our experience: whence do we come, and where are we going?"[5]

The various religions of humanity are also attempts to respond to these riddles.

They aren't a surrender to the temptation of idolatry; rather, they represent the difficult and uncertain but constant journey of human beings toward the ultimate and inexpressible mystery which encompasses our existence, whence we come and to which we are returning.

Someone once affirmed that thanks to this "mystery" people can understand one another and dialogue. We could thus invert a tendency which has had bitter consequences even in recent history: that of setting one country against another because of religion.

The "faces" of God

An irrepressible supplication to the transcendent abides in the human heart. This supplication is something like the leitmotif in a great symphony: although presented with various instruments and arrangements, it constitutes the unity of the symphony.

The "variations" on the theme are the various "faces" which this "inexpressible mystery" assumes in the religious map of the world. All religions, in fact, propose an image of God—that is, an image of that ultimate and first reality with which they are called to confront themselves in this life. The variety of faces should not make us forget the oneness of the mystery from which they stem and to which they refer.

Let us look at some of them briefly.

Brahman

For about 3,000 years, the first and ultimate Reality in the great river of Hinduism has been Brahman. In such religions as Hinduism, Buddhism, Chinese universism, Shintoism and the African religions...no word is used which means "God" in our sense.

Etymologically, Brahman means "that which is pronounced," that is, the effective word of the rite, but it is immediately used to indicate the magical power of the sacrificial rite, and thus the Absolute, the All.

A celebrated hymn of the *Regveda* (X, 129), conceals him under the features of "That One," who lies at the origin of everything and precedes the gods themselves, who belong to the order of all that came into being later:

"Then there was not non-being, there was not being.
There was no atmosphere, nor the heaven above.
What was moving? Under whose protection?
Was there the unfathomable, deep water?
Then, there was neither death nor immortality,
there was no sign of night or day;
That One breathed without breath on his own strength;
outside of him there was no other, nothing else.
There was darkness, everything was cloaked in darkness.
All was nothing but indistinct flickering;
then, that which was wrapped in emptiness, That One, emerging,
gave birth to himself with the power of his warmth."

The reflection on Brahman, on its nature and its relationship with being, tells the Catholic Church that in Hinduism "men contemplate the divine mystery and express it through an inexhaustible abundance of myths and through searching philosophical inquiry."[6]

Buddha

Buddhism has rejected the affirmations of Hinduism regarding the supreme Reality of the Brahman, together with any redeeming value of the idea of God. The basic preoccupation of this religion is to achieve freedom from pain.

The four noble truths of Buddha tend to help us understand why we suffer, for the purpose of removing the cause of suffering and suffering itself.

The figure of Buddha is placed above the gods and spirits that populate the universe. His law (*dharma*) and his cal forms of the Supreme Being: a theism of the woods, of the fields, of the heavens.

Yahweh

With Yahweh, the God of Abraham, of Isaac and of Jacob, we pass from the cosmic religions to the religions of historical, prophetic monotheism: Judaism, Islam and Christianity.

The hinge of these religions is the belief that God has intervened and has freely revealed himself in history through his envoys, in order to carry out his plan of salvation.

Judaism places the accent on the unity of God and the impossibility of depicting God in images. It knows the covenant offered by God to the Hebrew people, to whom he has entrusted the task of being his witnesses on earth. The Hebrew faith professes submission to God, but also and above all confidence, dialogue and the certainty that the covenant, once ratified, will never fail.

Here is a significant text on the identity of the Hebrew God:

"The Holy One—may he be blessed—said to Moses: 'What do you want to know? I am named according to my actions. At times I am called *El Shaddai* (omnipotent God), or *Zevoat* (Hosts), *Elohim* (God) or *YHWH* (Lord). When I judge humanity, I am called Elohim, when I make war against the wicked I am called Zevoat, when I put a stop to the sin of man I am called El Shaddai, when I have compassion on my world I am called YHWH, because the tetragrammaton [the four-letter name] signifies nothing other than mercy, as is said: "The Lord, the Lord, a God merciful and gracious..." (Ex 34:6). This is the meaning of the verse, 'ehjeh 'asher'ehjeh ("I am who I am": Ex 3:14): I am named according to my actions'" (Exodus Rabbah 3:6).

Allah

Like Judaism, Islam insists on the oneness of God and the impossibility of depicting him. But it emphasizes God's transcendence in such a radical way as to exclude any ethnic, priestly or ritual mediation. The Prophet has simply recorded and transmitted to men God's sovereign will. (The Christian message, instead, extends the concept of the covenant to the point of announcing God's real self-communication to humanity in the person of Jesus Christ. Jesus becomes the principle of the interpersonal communion between God and humanity and of persons among themselves—Jn 1:1-18.)

Allah is the center of the Islamic faith, and for Moslems there is no public act that does not begin "in the name of the gracious and merciful God."

Here are two citations from chapters (sura) of the *Koran:*

"In the name of God, gracious and merciful!" "Say: 'He, God is one—God, the eternal—He did not bring forth, nor was he brought forth—and no one is his equal' (Sura 112, of the "Sincere worship," 1-4).

"God! There is no other God then he, the Living One, who exists of himself. He never slumbers nor sleeps; to him belongs everything in the heavens and everything on the earth. Who could ever intercede with him without his permission? He knows what is before them and behind them, while they do not possess his knowledge except as he wills. He sets his throne over the heavens and the earth, nor does he tire in watching over them. He is the Most High, the Almighty!" (Sura 2)

A god "according to my taste"

At this point someone might say: different peoples, different histories, different gods....

If this is how things are, there is not one God. Then, is God just a product of culture? Does every nation or every person make its own god?

We may also reason in this other way: the inner urge toward the inexpressible mystery belongs to every person and every people; the search for a transcendent being cannot be suppressed. But the *name* that persons and peoples give to God—if they don't accept or don't know the biblical, monotheistic and prophetic revelation—is a cultural fact bound to the history (personal and/or collective), to the place, to the environment, to the time and to the social and economic conditions in which the people live.

The encounter with the one true God (in the Christian faith, salvation) is possible to those who with an upright conscience are faithful to the dictates of their own religion (the system of beliefs and practices by which they honor that particular god). In fact, says Vatican II, "those also can attain salvation who through no fault of their own do not know the Gospel of Christ or his Church, yet sincerely seek God, and moved by grace strive by their deeds to do his will as it is known to them through the dictates of conscience."[7]

But other attitudes are also common today—promoted by the ease and rapidity of communication.

These attitudes are: a subjective attitude regarding God and the faith, atheism, indifference, religion reduced to social and/or political convenience, syncretism or the uncritical mixing of the elements of different religions, rigid fundamentalism, adherence to sects....

When we look closely at these attitudes, the temptation to idolatry is not alien to them. In fact, such attitudes do not foster the awareness of human limitations and the journey toward the mystery of the one God, made known in Jesus Christ.

All are called and obliged to search for this truth.

Summary of the Cosmic Religions

Religion	Geographic area	Concept of God	Concept of man
Hinduism	India-Pakistan Bangladesh	* Polytheistic religion * Many divinities among whom are the triad Brahman (creator), Visnù (preserver), Shiva (destroyer) * Concept of reincarnation * Subdivision into castes * See: sacred Hindu texts	* The soul of man transmigrates and is reborn according to the actions performed in life
Buddhism	Tibet-China Japan Southeast Asia	* Preached by Buddha (565 B.C.): religion understood as an instrument of liberation and salvation for man * The doctrine does not deepen the study about God, and negates every liberating value of the idea of God	* Man is considered above all in relationship to suffering and death * Search for the means to suppress suffering by means of the following four truths: 1) origin of suffering (birth, illness, old age, death) 2) suffering = consequence of desire, of pleasure, of attachment to existence 3) overcoming suffering by means of detachment from desire (Nirvana) 4) ignorance, source of suffering; conscience, means of overcoming suffering
Confucianism	China	* Founded by Confucius in the sixth century before Christ * Polytheistic religion * The highest divinity is heaven (Tien) who presides in the Temple (the Temple of Heaven in Peking)	* Man is obliged to practice virtue, which makes him a superior person * Striving for improvement, of oneself and of society

Taoism	Japan China	* Tao is the principle of everything to which man tends	* Man strives for immortality, that is, the attainment of divinity (Tao) through the constant improvement of self and passive adaptation to natural laws * Opposition to any form of social organization * Return to the Tao = return to the profound roots of the human person * Mystical experiences and ecstasies, considered to be anticipation of future immortality
Traditional Religions	Africa	* Supreme being similar to the "heaven" of ancient Chinese tradition; is identified with nature	* Man is subject to the Supreme Being on whom he totally depends as the "vital force" * Every place in nature is seen as a place of worship

Atheism of Yesterday, Atheism of Today

Some non-believers of yesterday rejected God in order to affirm themselves, their personality, their creativity and their will to power: theirs was a humanistic atheism.

Other people rejected God in order to free oppressed men and women: this was a social, revolutionary atheism.

Today history shows us what happens when we eliminate God in order to affirm and liberate the human person.

Nietzsche and Sartre, two masters of the first kind of atheism, affirmed "either God or man." They both arrived at a form of nihilism. Nietzsche's "superman" is destined for self-destruction. Sartre's "model man," freed from any dependence or limitation, reaches the awareness of "being-for-nothing," or "for death," or, as Sartre would say, of being a "useless passion."

Marxism, which took root in the countries of eastern Europe and in Russia especially, has shown how little liberation seventy years of atheism could produce.

How is the atheism of our contemporaries expressed? Not many are actively involved in trying to destroy the idea of God. Instead, a good number make attacks in open or subtle ways, so as to create a negative image of religion. Those who support the Church don't pay as much attention to its religious function as to the contribution the Church gives regarding issues that touch other institutions, such as peace, human rights, ecology, defense of the poor....

The militant atheism of yesterday has been replaced by indifference, which is manifested in various ways—some open, some disguised. Its strategy isn't to state that God does not exist, but rather to so act as not to pose the question. This indifference holds that human thought is too weak to fly so high; it affirms that the things that are important and decisive for humanity today are very different from belief in God....

It's very instructive to analyze the way in which religious indifference is present in daily life. Religious indifference involves care for one's appearance and image, so it's *superficiality*; it involves the exasperating search for advantages, especially economic advantages, so it's *possessiveness*. It includes the desire to derive as much immediate pleasure as possible from all one's experiences, which is *narcissism*. The individual affirms self at the expense of others and of the community, which is *individualism*. Any principle, objective norm or norm outside the conscience is rejected; thus, religious indifference is *exaggerated subjectivism* and the denial of any objective ethic.

The contemporary world has been shown that the elimination of faith does not produce the expected results (promotion of the person and justice). Yet from this brief description we can see that the elimination of faith continues to "kill" God, and even more so, religions. Now, however, it does so to achieve a new freedom, individual and subjective: that of enjoying life. This is an instrumental freedom because its ambition is to obtain happiness, or at least something that resembles it—for example, being well-to-do. This practical atheism—shared even by many believers because it's subtle and disguised—is characterized by the rejection of any principle outside the conscience capable of determining a morality that is valid for everyone, at all times. This is the triumph of subjectivity. Morality is what I decide in my conscience; there are no other gods besides me!

An important practical conclusion is that historical religions must be opposed as culturally out-dated and reactionary, for they believe that there is an objective ethic and they have the courage to propose it.

Evaluating the Questions so as to Grow in Freedom

"Through sin the person...rejects Christ and his plan for the new man, and betrays the task of serving his brothers and sisters, of transforming the world and of leading creation to praise the Creator."[8]

Views

Shapers of Twentieth-Century Thought

Karl Marx

We give this title to two thinkers who greatly influenced the culture of the past hundred years and longer, even with regard to the value and meaning religion has for humanity and for personal and social life. Their influence continues.

Marx (1818-1883) stated: "Religion is the sigh of the oppressed creature, the heart of a world without a heart, as it is the spirit of a world from which the spirit is excluded. It is the opium of the people."

This affirmation is not completely new and can also be expressed in other words: Landowners and the rich "use God" to establish and safeguard their own power and privi-

leges. Religion teaches obedience to those in authority, so it reinforces injustice. If we free people from economic, social and political slavery, there will be no more need for God, and religion will disappear.

Unforgettable events such as the "spring in Prague," of 1968—a popular movement for liberation from socialism, put down by Soviet troops that invaded Czechoslovakia; the 1989 "spring" in Peking, put down in a bloody massacre by the Chinese army; and the political turnover in Eastern Europe in 1989 and thereafter, call into question the Marxist theses.

For Reflection

Does Marx's judgment of religion as a "drug" and an instrument at the service of injustice and the dominant class relate more to historical experiences or to religion itself?

Do the events recalled here point an accusing finger at historical forms of Marxism or at the doctrine as such?

Does the Marxist "suspicion" about religion now have the "right of citizenship" or should it be called into question?

What should we say of believers who fervently nourish their faith in God but are indifferent to human progress and personal and community development?

Do human sufferings stem exclusively from socio-economic situations, or do they have their origin in the human condition itself?

Friedrich Nietzsche

Christianity has been described as a religion born of the initiative of God, which elevates us and gives us serenity and peace.

"A pity," said Nietzsche (1844-1900), "to thus annul the virile autonomy of the human person. In itself autonomy is not serene, nor a bearer of peace; it's insecure and, for this reason, fascinating.

"Faith in God alienates man: it doesn't allow him to grow or to affirm himself. Christianity raises 'weak men.'

"Man has a creative power; he is called to become a 'superman.' Why induce him to renounce it? 'God is dead'! God remains dead! And we have killed him."

Destroyers of God also destroy the world that believers have built: the symbols, the churches, the professions of faith, the catechisms, the ceremonies, the religious practices, Christian education....

Nietzsche did not construct a philosophical "system," but he spoke with the warmth and power of an artist. His ideas are an open school which many have been able to attend. To some he appeared as a prophet, the forerunner of a new and emancipated civilization; to others, the "perverse genius" of Nazism.

For Reflection

As a student of theology, Nietzsche came from a family of Protestant ministers; he rejected his faith and became "an atheist to save man." This can lead to many reflections. For example:

What happened to Nietzsche is re-enacted every time a young person who is raised in a very religious environment totally rejects what he or she has been taught. What motives might lie at the root of this behavior?

Is removing God an indispensable condition for promoting, affirming and freeing the human person?

Today we speak of "indifference" more than of a denial of God. What problems do these two positions pose for the Christian?

Is the relationship between religion and the promotion of the person important for an authentic religion? What type of religion is put forward by the phenomena of religious sects, of fundamentalism, of the return to natural religions? How do these resolve the relationship between religion and human promotion?

Views

Like Water from a Source

God has left a trace of himself in the heart of the human person, and the person, imprinted with a nostalgia for the Absolute, seeks God—or rather, seeks a living word no longer hidden in the riddles of existence. Where do we find it?

In the following interview, Cardinal Carlo Martini leads us to a wellspring—the word of God, the Gospel.

How does God call people? What do you remember about the beginning of your vocation?

"I would have to point to two moments: that of my religious choice, which goes back a long way; this was the first intuition that God is everything and can ask everything.... But I'm aware that after many years I rediscovered somewhat the evangelizing aspect, what it means to bring the good news among the people of the world. Until this revelation I lived [my religion] by learning and memorizing...then I found a more personal manner, like water gushing from a spring."

What do people expect from the Church?

"Let me say rather what I would like to bring to others. I would try to help them share in the hope that I receive from the words of the New Testament...."

What can we learn from the Bible?

"Everything. Those fundamental realities which make it possible to overcome our anxiety about the last things and to dedicate ourselves to our neighbor with freedom of heart; the certainty that God forms a people which grows throughout history and in which we are called to take part."

Some people look for salvation from the young; others, from human genius—in the ability to adapt, to invent new ways. What is your opinion?

"I find salvation in the Gospel."[9]

For Reflection

How does God "call" people? In our life's journey, how much importance should we give to the search each of us carries on within him/herself, and how much importance to listening to the word of God, especially the Gospel?

What do you expect from the Church?

What has the word of God given you? How important is it for you?

Views

Life: An Adventure in Which Everything Is at Stake

"A young man and woman meet, come to know one another, love one another. They discover that they understand one another, simply and immediately, that they find in one another the meaning and fullness of life that they were unconsciously looking for. They are surprised and grateful for what is happening to them. They plan their future, their life together, and it seems rich in promise and almost without shadows.

"However, when the future becomes present, when life together becomes a daily experience, and the plan in which all their hopes were placed begins to translate into the complicated plot of social relationships, then the difficult and uncertain aspects of love emerge. Unforeseen obstacles appear which hinder a full and unconditional mutual openness. Sometimes there is even the temptation to mutual doubt and suspicion.

"What should we say, then? That the time of engagement was an illusion, a Saturday that was never followed by the day of celebration? This cynical and skeptical conclusion is only a variation of that common saying: marriage is the grave of love. The practical consequence of this viewpoint is escape into the abstract experience of 'romantic love,' into an irresponsible relationship formed alongside what is called 'normal life,' into a sentimental game in which persons lack the courage to make concrete social choices.

"But this is not the only option. The other option is to recognize that while marriage between man and woman is one of the most meaningful and enriching experiences, it is not yet that ultimate fullness that all persons seek. Like most life in common, their life together is an adventure in which everything is continually at stake. To find the courage to begin each day anew, the love between man and woman needs to give up the illusion of being the ultimate reality that can justify all of one's existence. On the contrary, this love has to be lived as the partial, yes, but real and promising beginning of a pledge and a hope in which the couple finds the strength to overcome every trial."[10]

For Reflection

What place should God have in daily life, so that this existence doesn't become "a Saturday that is never followed by the day of celebration"?

What obstacles do we need to overcome and what attitudes do we need to foster in ourselves, so that the gift of faith may inspire, sustain and direct our daily life?

As the text says, life together as husband and wife is one of the richest and most meaningful of human experiences. How can it be kept this way?

Can human love justify all of one's existence?

This quotation reminds us believers of our obligation to live every relationship in "a full and unconditional mutual openness." What conditions are needed for this to happen?

Views

Can "Providence" Reach Us Through the Stars?

"Those who believe that stars direct a person's actions and passions and the good or the evil that he or she does—all without the intervention of God—must be silenced. This theory conflicts with the Christian concept of divinity."

St. Augustine wrote these words in *The City of God* three centuries after Christ. He himself had felt the fascination of astrology, but had begun to doubt it when he discovered that a rich landowner and his slave had been born under the same sign of the zodiac, at exactly the same moment.

Well-founded problems have been raised by theologians with regard to astrology.

If astrology presents itself as a religion and belief, opposed to Christianity, and, worse yet, if it pretends to affirm that every last detail of human destinies on earth has been written in the heavens, a Christian cannot help but take offense. Such astrology reduces the human person to a marionette directed by the threads of the stars. It denies free will and automatically negates sin together with the necessity for the salvation brought by Christ. Astrology can attack the very basis of Christianity.

For Reflection

Does Providence reach us through the stars?

When can astrological faith become an idol for a Christian?

Let's Celebrate the Lord Our God

O heavenly beings, give glory to his name.
Ascribe to the Lord, O heavenly beings,
ascribe to the Lord glory and strength.
Ascribe to the Lord the glory of his name;
worship the Lord in holy splendor.
The voice of the Lord is over the waters;
the God of glory thunders,
the Lord over mighty waters.
The voice of the Lord is powerful;
the voice of the Lord is full of majesty.
The voice of the Lord breaks the cedars;
the Lord breaks the cedars of Lebanon.
He makes Lebanon skip like a calf,
and Sirion like a young wild ox.
The Lord sits enthroned over the flood;
the Lord sits enthroned as king forever.
May the Lord give strength to his people!
May the Lord bless his people with peace!

(Psalm 29)

Witness

Edith Stein

Edith Stein (1891-1942) was born into a practicing Jewish family. At eighteen, she became an agnostic and affirmed that it is impossible to believe in the existence of God. At thirty, she asked to be baptized, and when she was forty-five she pronounced her religious vows in a Carmelite monastery. She had not yet reached the age of fifty-one when she died in a gas chamber at the Auschwitz concentration camp.

On May 1, 1987, Pope John Paul II declared her blessed.

Her history is a mysterious journey toward the God of Jesus Christ.

Edith was very intelligent and well-educated. She knew seven languages. At eighteen she was the only woman enrolled in the courses of German, history and philosophy in her city. When she was twenty-one, she transferred to the university of Göttingen, attracted by the teaching of Edmund Husserl, the founder of phenomenology. She became his best student and assistant.

She was not only a woman "taken up with study." She also had a great love for the poor. She was on the side of the first workers to strike, and had a great feminine sensitivity that places her close to Simone Weil (1909-1943), a Jewish woman of France who drew close to Christianity without ever receiving baptism. Once she became a Christian, Edith explored the vocation of woman in her writings and conferences.

The young Edith had a passion for research and threw herself into the study of phenomenology with enthusiasm. "I was twenty years old," she wrote, "and full of expectation. Psychology had disappointed me; I had reached the conclusion that it was a science still in its infancy, lacking in objective foundations. Instead, the little I knew about phenomenology enchanted me, especially its objective working method."

Her openness to truth was revealed in her encounters with Max Scheler, a Christian professor. Edith writes of him: "For me, as for many others, his influence went far beyond the sphere of philosophy.... He overflowed with Christian ideas and knew how to present them in a brilliant way, with power and persuasion. For me it was the revelation of a universe totally unknown until then. While this revelation did not yet lead me to the faith, it opened up to me an area of phenomena that I couldn't ignore.... And so the barriers of rationalism, in which I had been unknowingly educated, fell away and I suddenly found myself face to face with the world of faith."

Journey toward conversion

Why didn't this woman in search of truth, an intelligent and sensitive modern woman, return to the God of the Hebrews, since she had been born into an orthodox and practicing Jewish family?

It's not easy to answer that question. Mystery surrounds any spiritual event.

Edith's mother twice posed this same question: once on the occasion of Edith's baptism and again when she entered Carmel.

The first time the mother didn't understand, and she wept in great suffering, leaving her daughter quite upset. Twelve years later she continued the discussion: it was October 12, 1933, Edith's feastday. Edith had decided to spend a day with the family. She accompanied her mother to the synagogue and followed the rites. On the way home, the following dialogue took place.

Mother: "Didn't you like the sermon of the rabbi? Wasn't he right in what he said? You can be a religious person also as a Jew."

Daughter: "Yes, if you don't know anything else."

Mother: "And you, why did you come to know him? I don't have anything against him. He may have been a very good man, but why did he want to make himself equal to God?"

We can trace Edith's journey to some extent. It was a mystery of grace and therefore a free gift from the Lord, who made use of some concrete instruments: the encounter with suffering lived in a Christian way; participation in the liturgy; and finally, contact with the mystics through her studies.

For some time, Edith had been friends with Anna and Adolph Reinach; the latter had been her professor and was an assistant to Husserl. He too was Hebrew by birth, and was making a journey of faith, together with his wife. In the summer of 1916, they asked for Christian baptism.

In November, 1917, Professor Reinach was killed in the war. The suffering of the young wife, wrung by sorrow but at the same time comforted by the strength of Christ, left a strong impression on Edith. Later, as a Carmelite, she wrote: "That was my encounter with the cross, with the divine power that the cross gives to those who carry it. For the first time the Church visibly appeared to me, born of the passion of Christ and victorious over death."

Her journey toward faith continued, thanks to some friends who brought her to attend both Protestant and Catholic liturgies. She did not understand the Eucharist, but it commanded her respect.

The study of phenomenology led her to read the writings of the mystics, among them St. Teresa of Avila. Her conversion came about while she read St. Teresa's autobiography in the home of friends. Here is her own account: "I casually took a book from the library, *The Life of St. Teresa, Recounted by Herself.* I began to read it and couldn't put it down until I had finished. When I closed the book, I said, 'This is the truth.'"

She had spent the night reading. In the morning she went to look for a catechism and missal. And so she began her instruction in the faith that had suddenly been enkindled in her.

Holocaust

This doctor in philosophy was baptized on January 1, 1922, at thirty years of age. She received the name Teresa Hedwig: Teresa, in gratitude to the saint; Hedwig, out of love for her godmother, the woman who had offered her friendship and hospitality during that period.

A decade later she was dismissed from her teaching position because of the anti-Semitic laws enforced by the Nazis. In 1933, she became a postulant at the Carmel in Cologne, and in 1935 she pronounced her religious vows. Her faith was expressed in acts of charity and growth in the spiritual life.

In 1942 the Nazi troops took her from the Carmelite monastery in Holland, where the sisters had offered her protection, and deported her to Auschwitz, together with her sister Rosa. Rosa was the only member of her family who understood her. She too had been baptized. She was Edith's companion in the concentration camp and in death.

August 9, 1942, was most probably the day that Edith entered the gas chamber, offering her life for her suffering people.[11]

Notes

1. Buzzati, D. "Racconto di Natale," in *La boutique del mistero*. Milan: Mondadori, 1988, pp. 96-98.

2. CEB. *Il libro della fede*. Milan: Edizioni Paoline, 1988.

3. *Dizionario di teologia biblica*. Turin: Marietti, 1971, p. 531.

4. Rossano, P. "Alle fonti dell'esperienza religiosa" in *Jesus, XI,* 1989, n. 4, Supplemento (Cristianesimo II), p. 100.

5. Vatican II. *Declaration on the Relation of the Church to Non-Christian Religions (Nostra Aetate)*. Boston: Pauline Books & Media, 1965, n. 1.

6. *Ibid.*, n. 2.

7. Vatican II. *Dogmatic Constitution on the Church (Lumen Gentium)*. Boston: Pauline Books & Media, 1964, n. 16.

8. CEI. *Signore, da chi andremo?* Rome: 1981.

9. Biagi, E. *Quante storie*. Milan: 1989, pp. 103-105.

10. CEI. *Non di solo pane*, Rome: 1979, pp. 33-34.

11. See De Mirabel, E. *Edith Stein, dall'università al lager di Auschwitz*. Milan: Edizioni Paoline, 1987.

About the Authors

Joseph Anfossi was ordained a priest in 1959. He is head of Pastoral Action for Families and Young People, diocese of Turin.

Fr. John Villata is head of the Study Center in the diocesan Office for Pastoral Action for Young People, diocese of Turin.

About this Series

These booklets are intended to help today's young (and not-so-young) adult explore how the ten commandments and eight beatitudes relate to human life and divine realities: How and where do they fit into contemporary culture and God's plan for us? The editors hope that *Reflections on the Commandments* will stimulate both deeper reflection and further research.

Booklets in this series: I Am the Lord Your God; You Shall Not Have Strange Gods Before Me; You Shall Not Take the Lord's Name in Vain; Remember to Keep Holy the Lord's Day; Honor Your Father and Your Mother; You Shall Not Kill; You Shall Not Commit Adultery, Nor Covet Your Neighbor's Wife; You Shall Not Steal, Nor Covet Your Neighbor's Goods; You Shall Not Bear False Witness; Blessed Are the Poor in Spirit.

St. Paul Book & Media Centers

ALASKA
750 West 5th Ave., Anchorage, AK 99501; 907-272-8183

CALIFORNIA
3908 Sepulveda Blvd., Culver City, CA 90230; 310-397-8676
5945 Balboa Ave., San Diego, CA 92111; 619-565-9181
46 Geary Street, San Francisco, CA 94108; 415-781-5180

FLORIDA
145 S.W. 107th Ave., Miami, FL 33174; 305-559-6715

HAWAII
1143 Bishop Street, Honolulu, HI 96813; 808-521-2731

ILLINOIS
172 North Michigan Ave., Chicago, IL 60601; 312-346-4228

LOUISIANA
4403 Veterans Memorial Blvd., Metairie, LA 70006; 504-887-7631

MASSACHUSETTS
50 St. Paul's Ave., Jamaica Plain, Boston, MA 02130; 617-522-8911
Rte. 1, 885 Providence Hwy., Dedham, MA 02026; 617-326-5385

MISSOURI
9804 Watson Rd., St. Louis, MO 63126; 314-965-3512

NEW JERSEY
561 U.S. Route 1, Wick Plaza, Edison, NJ 08817; 908-572-1200

NEW YORK
150 East 52nd Street, New York, NY 10022; 212-754-1110
78 Fort Place, Staten Island, NY 10301; 718-447-5071

OHIO
2105 Ontario Street, Cleveland, OH 44115; 216-621-9427

PENNSYLVANIA
510 Holstein Street, Bridgeport, PA 19405; 610-277-7728

SOUTH CAROLINA
243 King Street, Charleston, SC 29401; 803-577-0175

TENNESSEE
4811 Poplar Ave., Memphis, TN 38117; 901-761-2987

TEXAS
114 Main Plaza, San Antonio, TX 78205; 210-224-8101

VIRGINIA
1025 King Street, Alexandria, VA 22314; 703-549-3806

GUAM
285 Farenholt Ave., Suite 308, Tamuning, Guam 96911; 671-649-4377

CANADA
3022 Dufferin Street, Toronto, Ontario, Canada M6B 3T5; 416-781-9131